PHOTO
insights

Other books as author and photographer,
or as author

Photography: History, Art, Technique
Photography - the Definitive Visual History
Photo Judging
Picture Editing
Ang's World
Photo Field Guide
Creativity for Everyone
Digital Photography Step by Step
Digital Photography Essentials
Digital Photographer's Handbook
Complete Digital Photography
Questions & Angswers
Digital Photography: an Introduction
The Complete Photographer
Digital Photography Masterclass
Fundamentals of Photography
Digital Photography Through The Year
How To Photograph Absolutely Everything
Digital Photography
Tao of Photography
Eyewitness Companion: Photography
Picture Editing
Photoshop CS For Photography
Dictionary of Photography and Digital Imaging
Digital Photography
Silver Pixels
Kiss Digital Photography
Advanced Digital Photography
Complete Digital Photography
Private Album
Digital Video Handbook
Digital Video: An Introduction

As photographer

General Wade's Roads
Dorset
Marco Polo Expedition
Joy of Sex

PHOTO

wisdom, aphorism, truism

insights

TOMANG

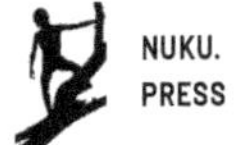

NUKU.
PRESS

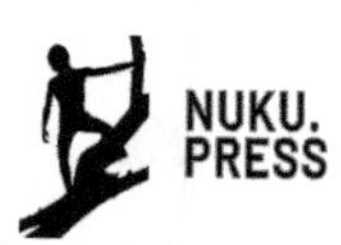

Contents

The why and the how

Writing more than two thousand words a day on photography - sometimes for months on end - you get to think a lot about images, cameras, and the photographic process. I've been doing just that for much of my 40+ years' working life.

After those millions of long-form words, it's natural that a few stay in the mind. Like a tune that you hum after a symphony concert, the fragment is only a handful of atoms from an hour of orchestral sounds, yet it is what is gifted to you by the music. It's what you keep in your heart and mind.

I've been composing insights, aphorisms on art and photography for many years. I like to think they're all you need to know about photography. The rest is just the mechanics of camera, lens and software operation. These are the gems vibrating at the heart of all the books I've written.

I suggest it's best to treat this book like a box of chocolates: pick one or two that take your fancy, but too many at once will give you indigestion. Before long, however, I hope you'll be back for more.

Tom Ang
Sony Digital Imaging Ambassador
Auckland 2021
www.tomang.com

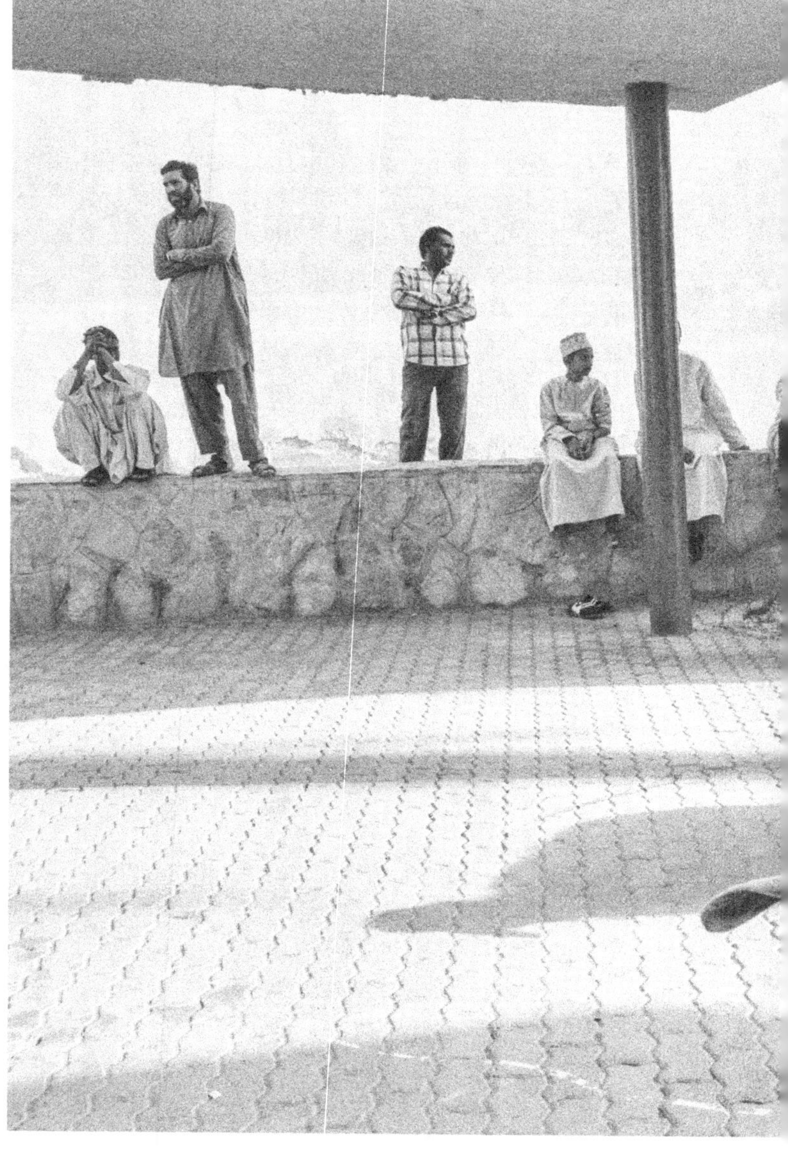

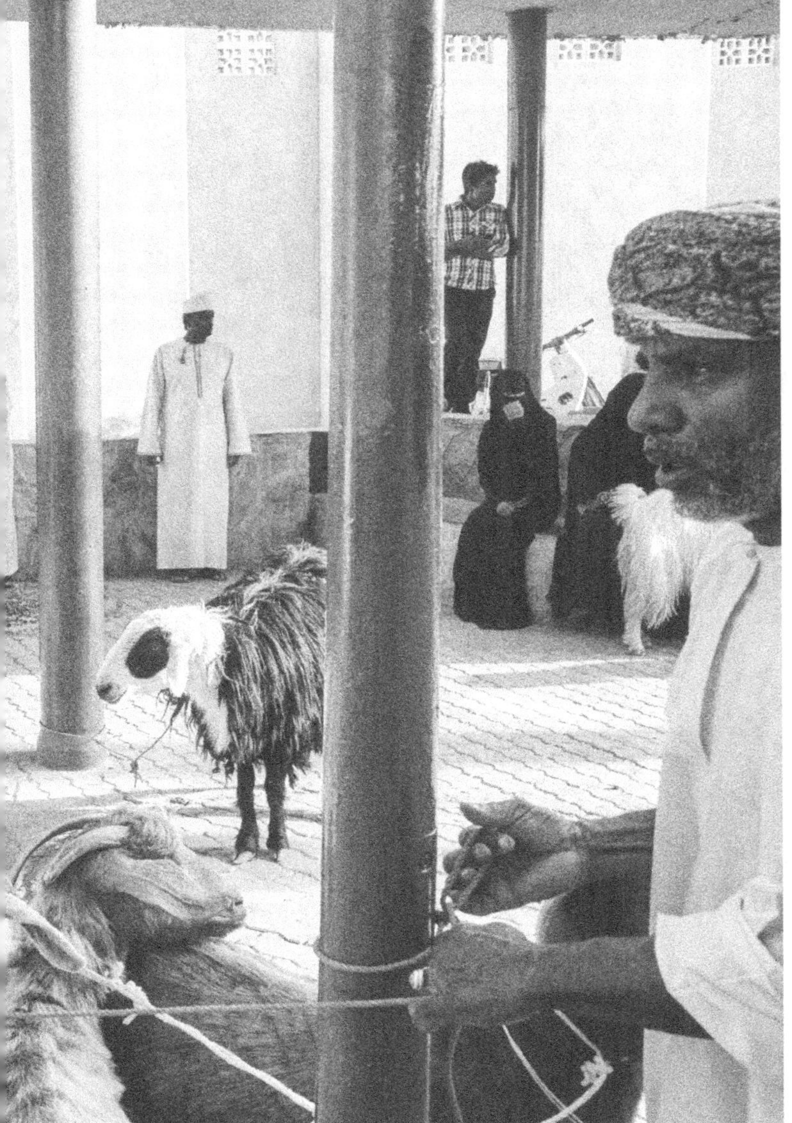

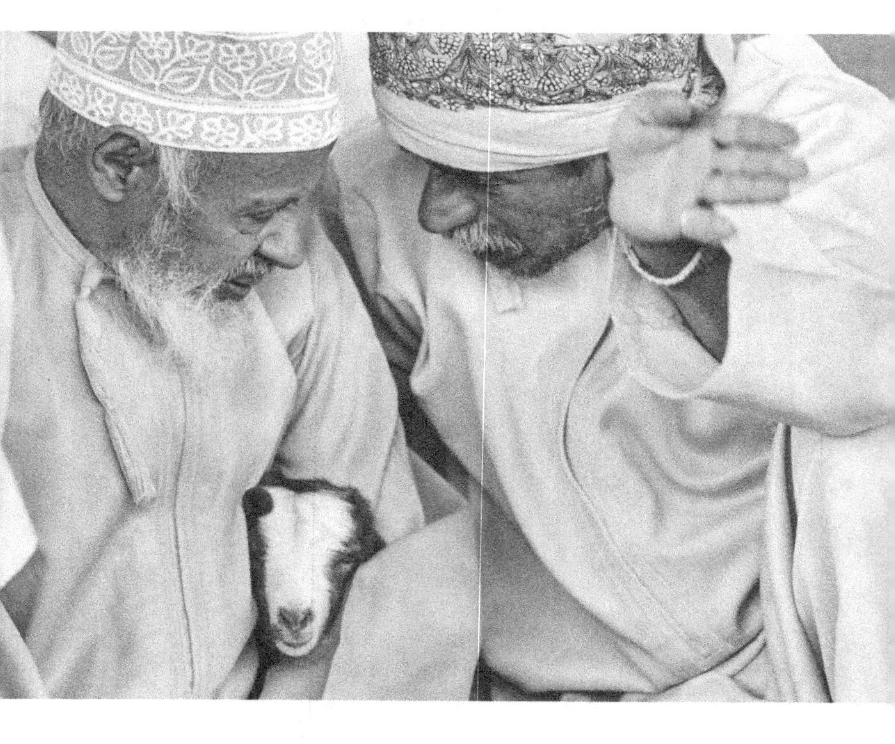

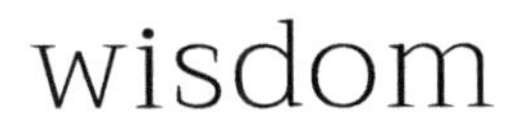

wisdom

The difference between 'good' and 'great' is a moment's inattention.

SMALL VISION seeks out great things; great vision is content with small things.

Lighting in photography is very easy ... if you work with what you're given.

A photograph is a **cipher**
to which we bring our
own **code books.**

To love **what you see** and to
photograph what you love:
what **else** is **there?**

An image's **story** enables
the present **to reach the**
future.

When **framing**, small differences **make** big differences.

ALWAYS have your camera within reach: **you get only one chance.**

DON'T SPOIL IT by thinking: simply *click* when the picture clicks within you.

A missed **shot is** serendipity's **calling-card for the** unprepared.

YOU NEVER break rules in photography. **How can you break** something that doesn't exist?

THE IMAGING CHAIN is that thing hanging around **every photographer's neck.**

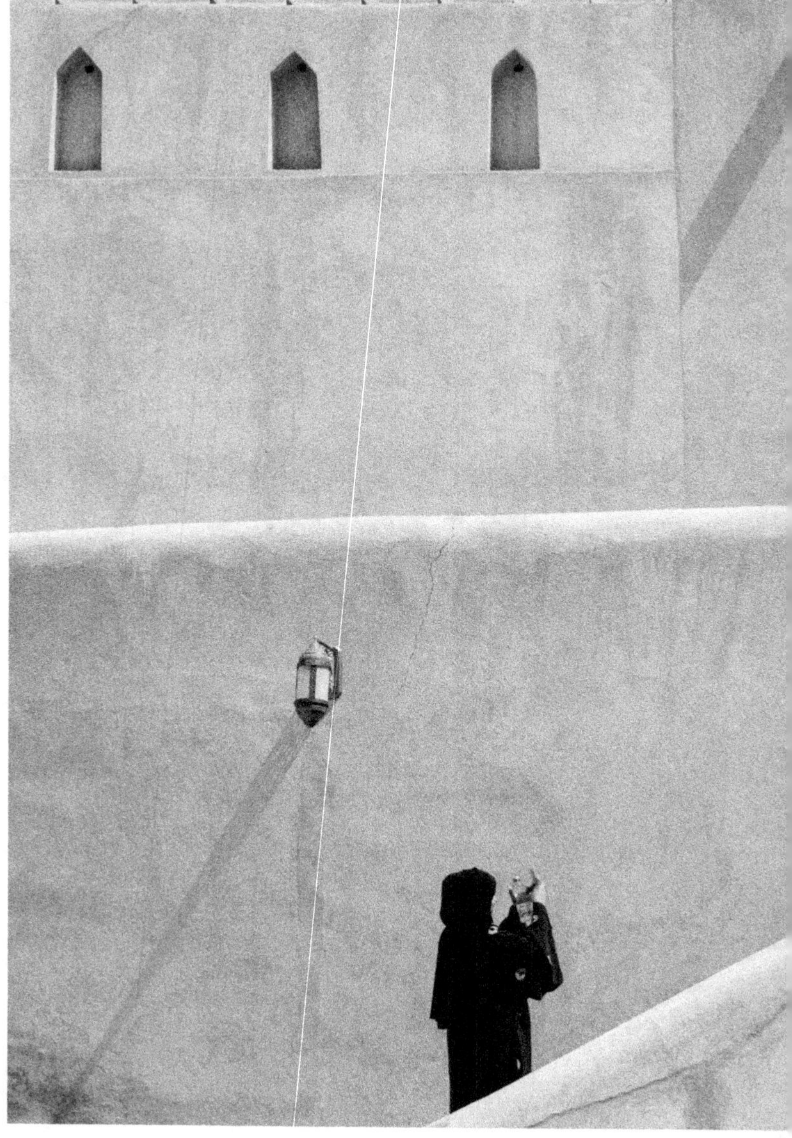

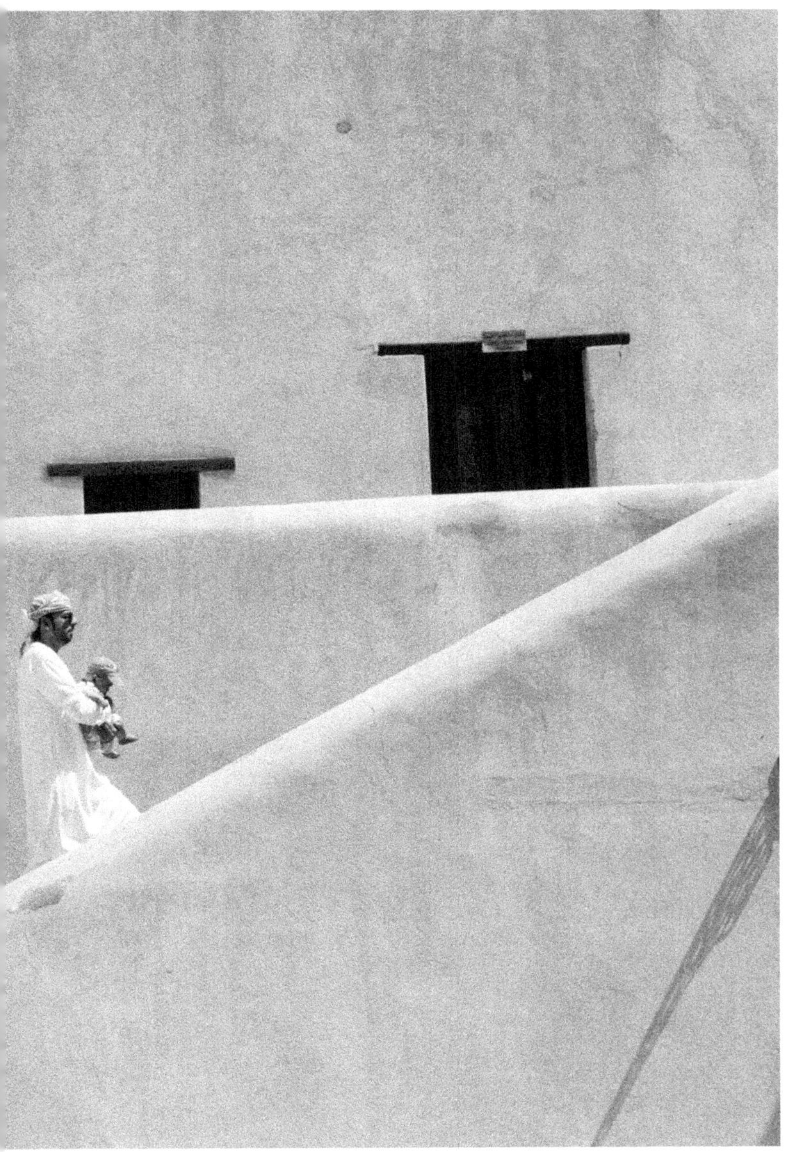

IN THE SAME WAY that water is
not an imperfect mirror, but
rather a *live **interpretation***
of its surroundings,
so photography is not an
imperfect record, but a continual,
conscious *appraisal* of all that
passes before its surface.

To be a
good documentary
photographer it helps to be
a **good fortune teller.**

When you next capture a fine
image, say '*Thank you*'.
It sets you up nicely for the
next.

THE BEST vantage points are where
no-one else goes.

Looking hard
obstructs seeing.

Cameras won't turn you into an artist, but can **transform** looking **into seeing.**

LOOK INTO the eyes of an image: if you don't see yourself in it, leave it.

The best luck comes to those who **prepare best.**

THERE ARE only *two* kinds of photograph: those you use, and those you don't.

Photographing landscapes is almost everything to do with what is inside you, and *almost nothing* to do with what is outside.

By feeling beyond what you can see, **you can see further than you can feel.**

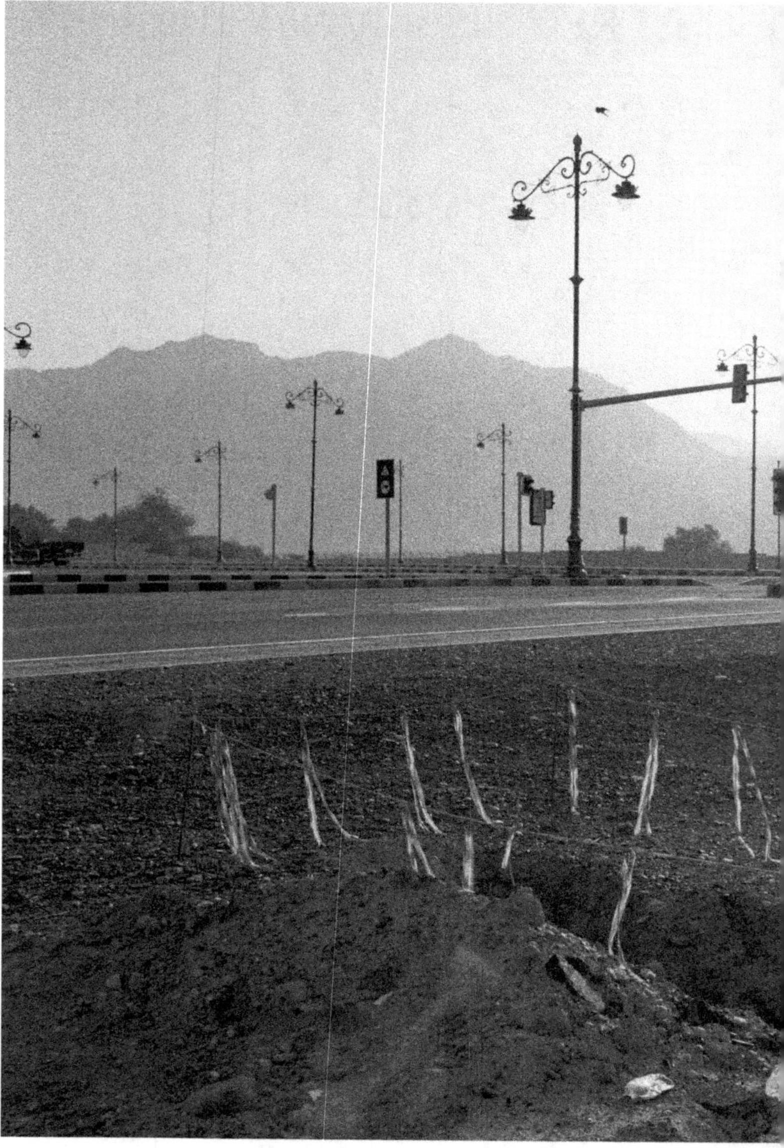

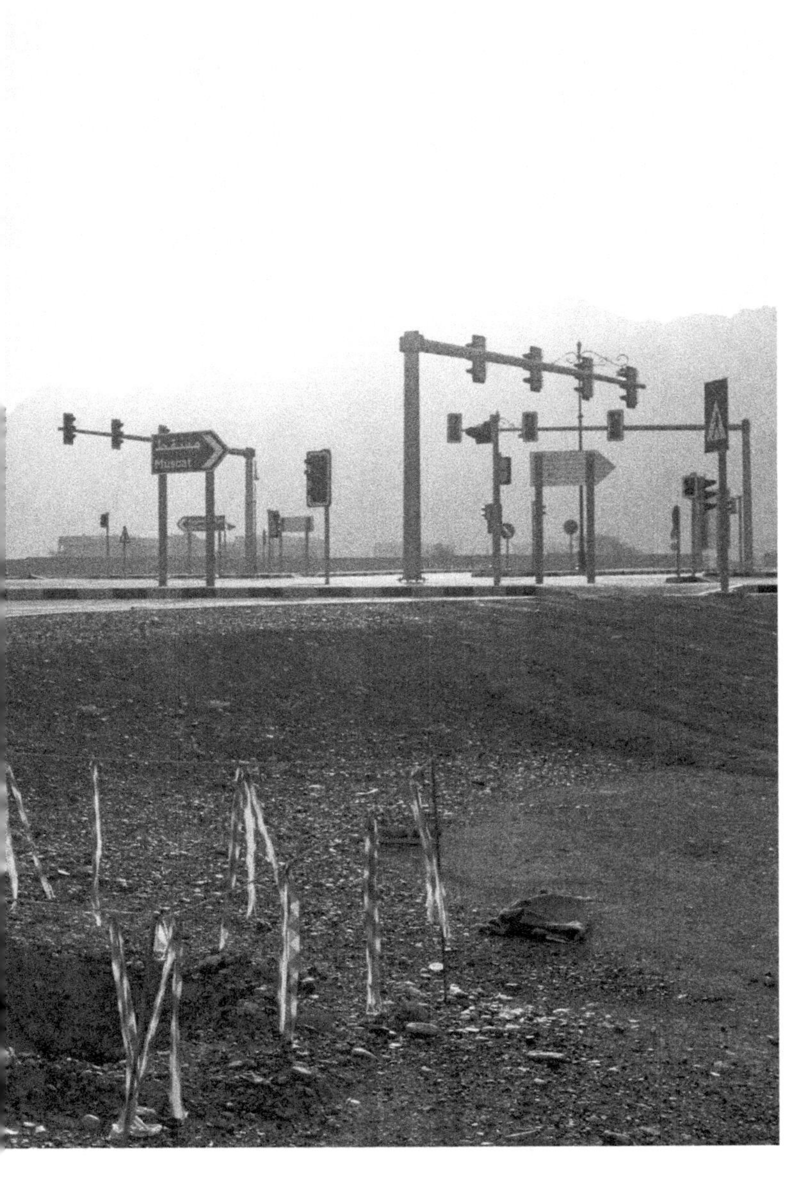

مسقط
Muscat

Photography **translates the** visible **into the** readable.

Eye-contact and a smile opens the door to **co-operation.**

The more deeply you feel, the more clearly **you can photograph.**

If you reject an image for
minor imperfections,
how can you
enjoy its **major delights?**

WHEN YOU **understand**

photography's illusion, you

see its **reality.**

It's all about what's **in the
image,** not what you can
get out of it.

If you're **comfortable**
making art, you're only
fooling around.

You miss **all of the**
shots you don't
expose.

Make every photograph
the first you've ever shot.

LOOKING FOR images is like looking for a lost object. If you don't know what you're looking for, **how do you know when you've found it?**

If working **hard** doesn't work, try **working** soft.

If your photographs don't depress you some of the time, **it's time to be harder on yourself.**

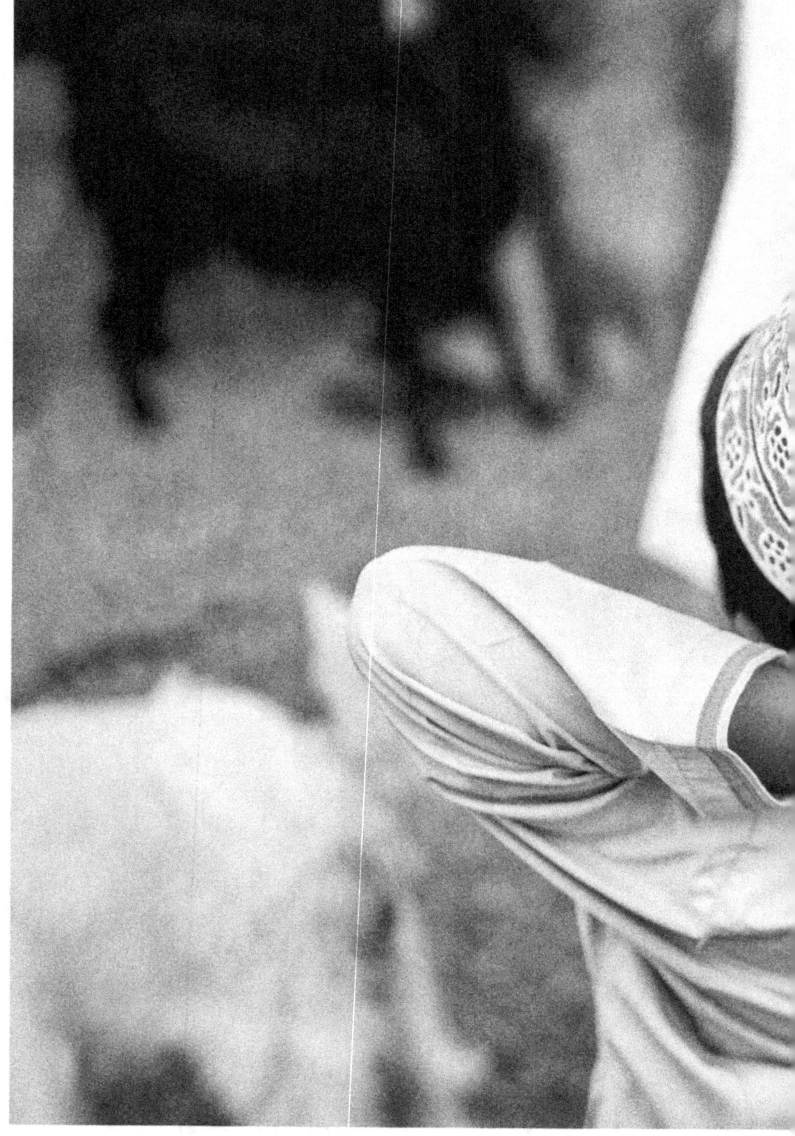

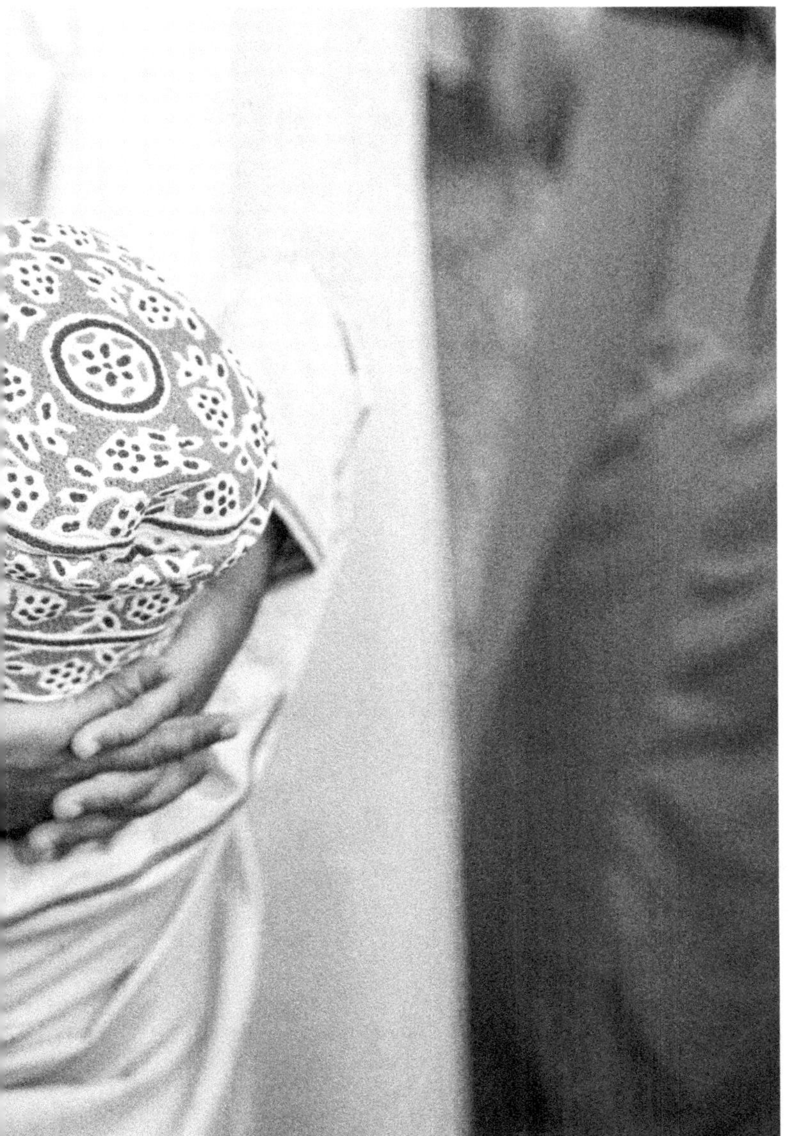

JUST AS ACTORS have to speak louder than feels natural, photographers have to get closer than is natural for the image to reach viewers.

Depth of field without depth of feeling is just empty space.

Photographic bliss is when outward image outshines inward eye.

Mastery means **knowing everything you need to,** then **forgetting it all** when you need to.

Where we stumble is where the treasure lies.

ANYONE can look at pictures, but it takes skill to see under them.

Everything you miss can be found in the gap between seeing and responding.

If you do not endow one of your images with **greater value** that others would, why are you keeping it?

If it's not a **'Hell, YES!'**, it's a 'Forget it'.

Success is measured by using
what you have
     on what you see
to produce the best you can.

Photography bullies time
into submission.

Photograph **what you
feel**, not what you see.

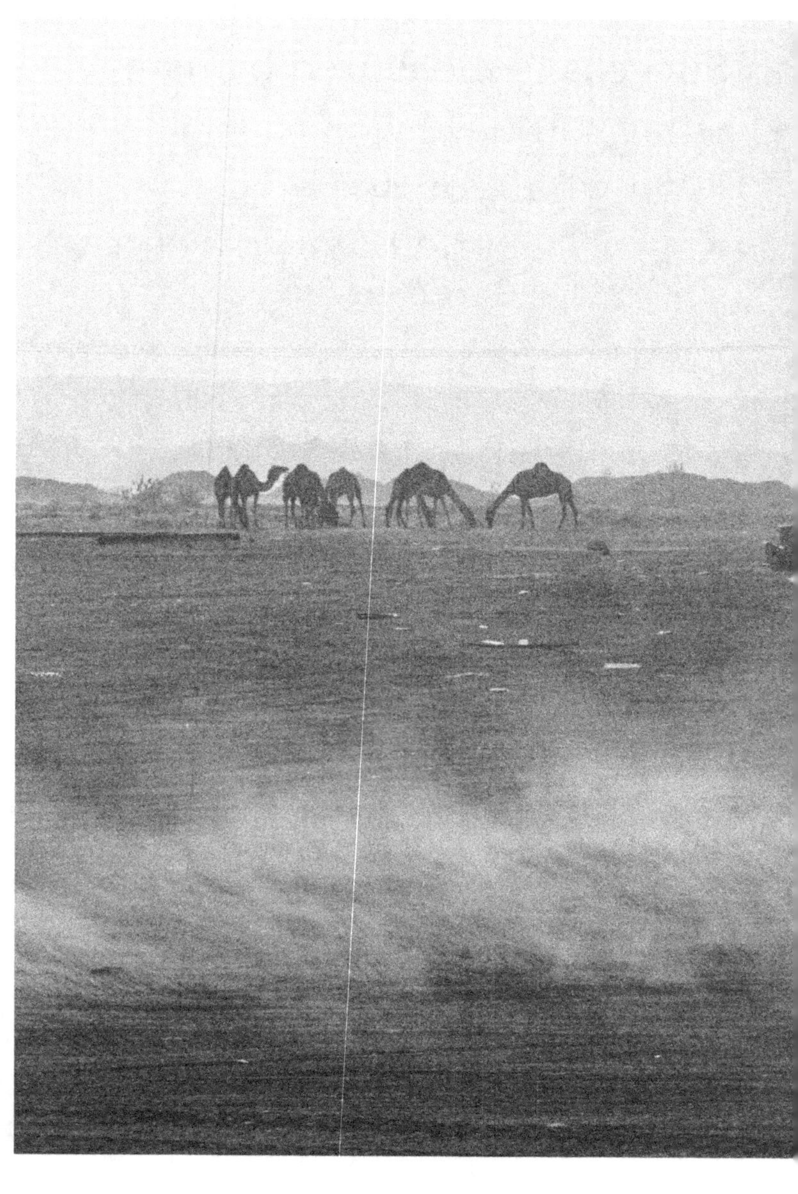

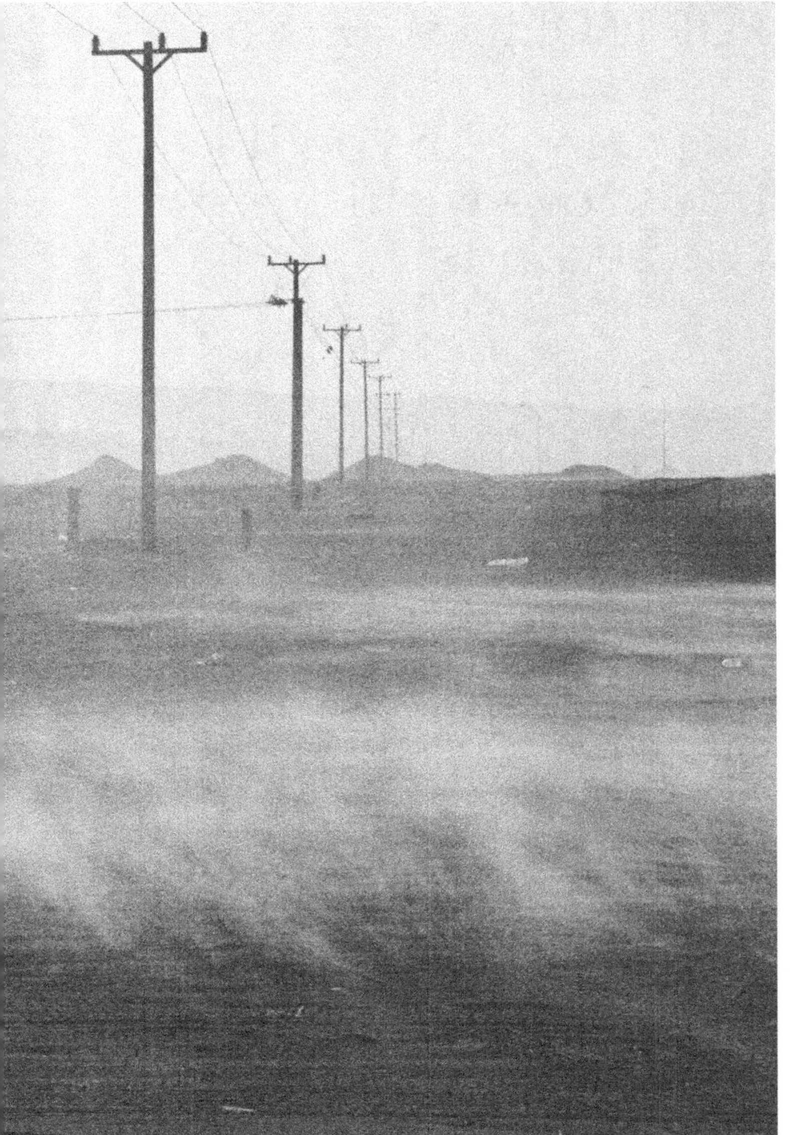

PORTFOLIO reviewing is the speed dating of photography: you'll know if it's love within two seconds.

Photography means 'write with light'; it doesn't mean 'fight with light'.

We must expose ourselves to life before we know how to expose the sensor to life.

A portrait is more than a depiction of a face, it is a record of your act of personal relating.

ALL light is good light; but some kinds are easier to work with than others.

Photographic style is showing what you want to show and to hell with what anyone else thinks.

CLOSE YOUR EYES the
better to feel; OPEN YOUR
HEART, the better to **see**.

Life is the **oxygen of**
photography,
your **sweat** is its **blood**.

Stills images are more

moving than **moving**

images.

MAKING A GREAT image
has it difficulties, but
ignoring the thousands of
others is the tricky bit.

That light in an image: it's
a reflection of your soul.

If you need encouragement
to become a photographer,
you'd best change plans.

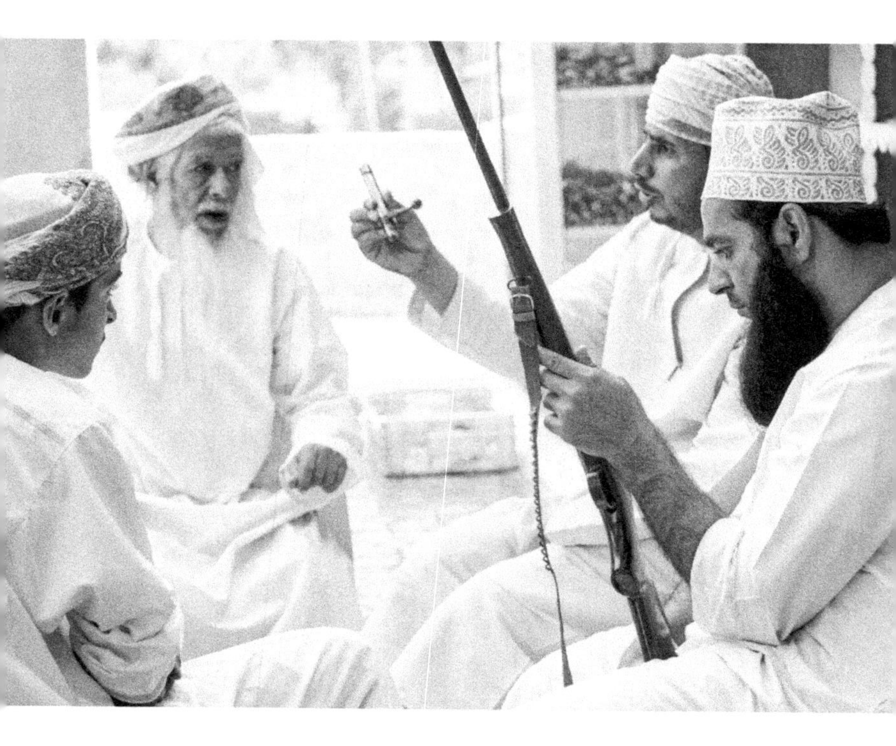

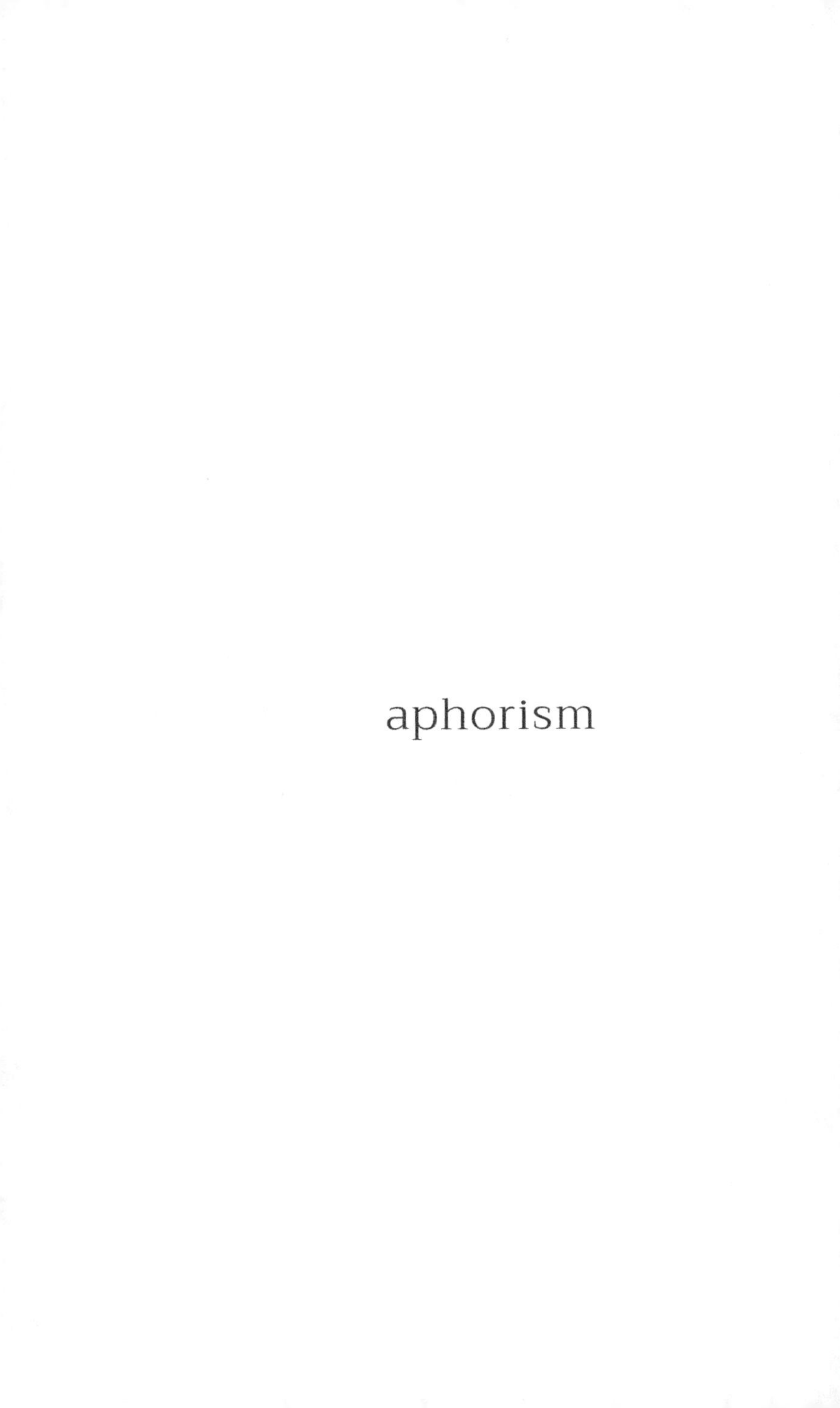

aphorism

Beauty is the Art of survival.

A photographer is one who dreams with both eyes open.

Photography grasps part of the present to prepare for the future.

You see **best** in silence.

Confusion is the door **that** opens to composition.

New moment, new thought; new thought, new image.

Your photographs record your dance with the world to life's tune.

A photograph is light filtered through your soul.

Exposure metering is expression metering.

A great landscape
**photograph gives a taste of
paradise.**

Making a photograph
records your intersection
with life.

THE WAY to catch a moment
is to move *at the
speed* of life.

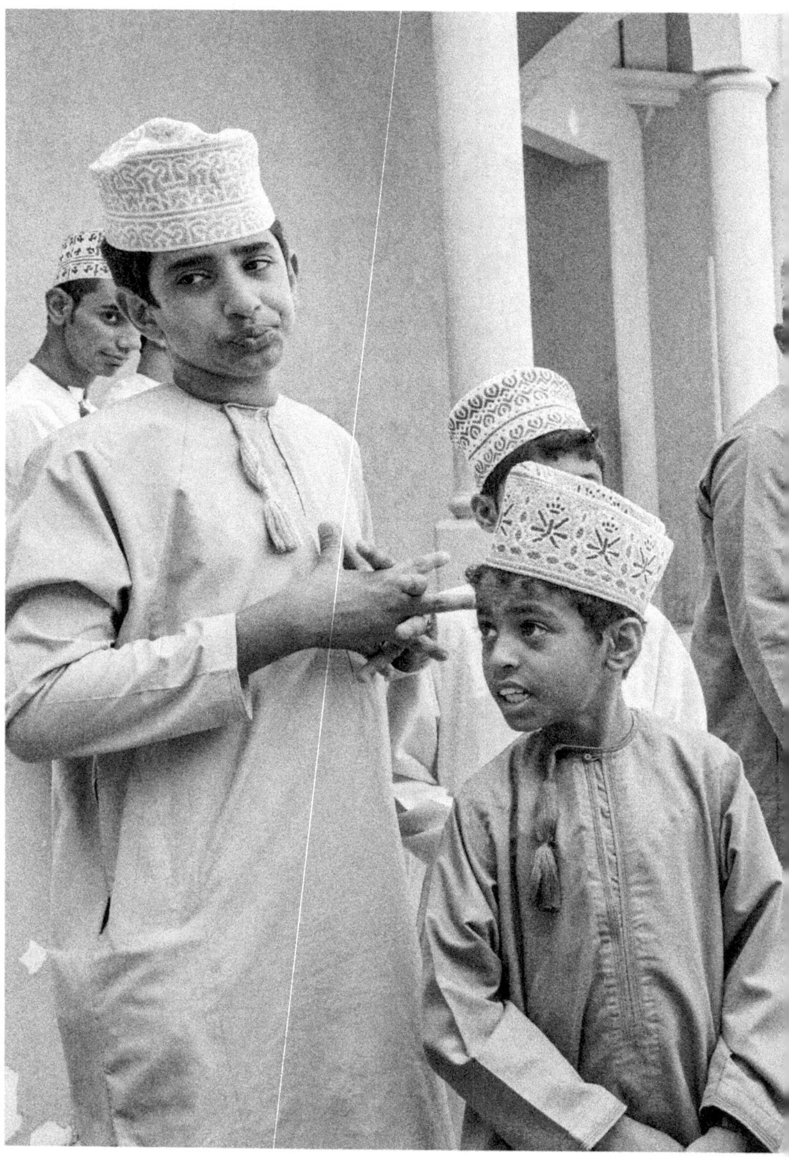

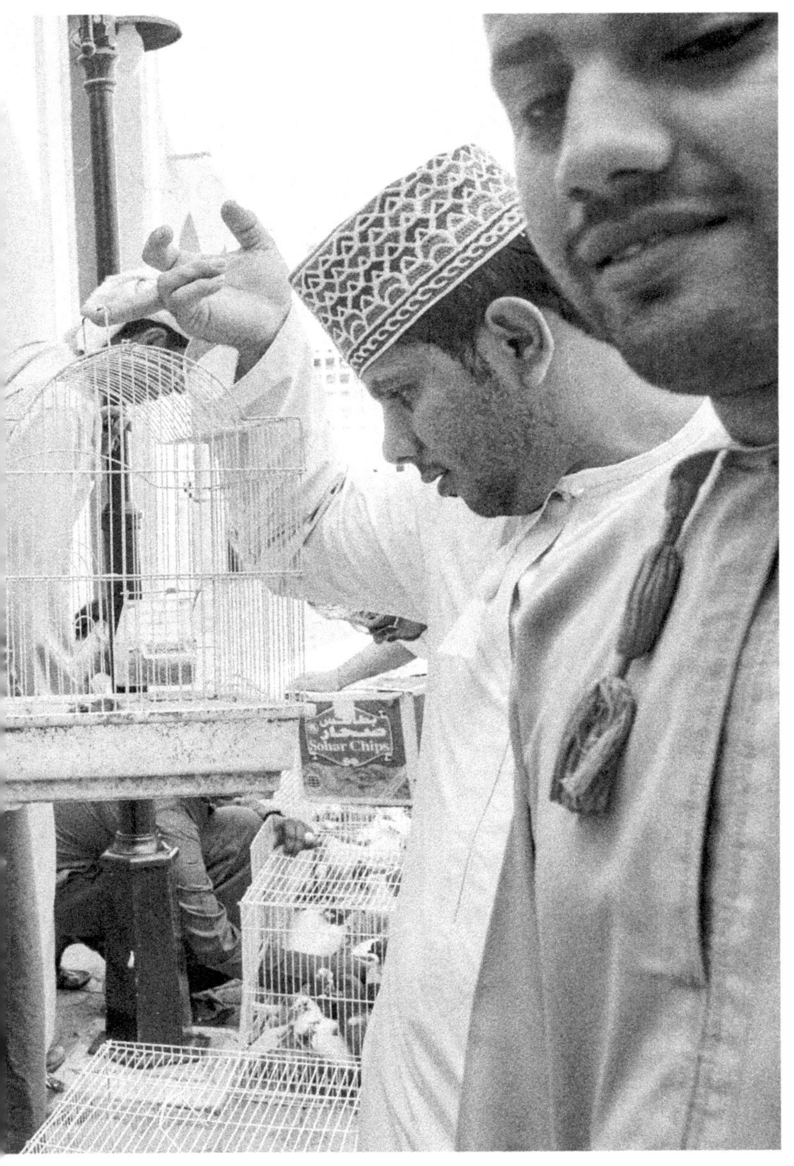

Bliss is when feeling, light and moment **embrace**.

If NECESSITY is the Mother of invention, then the Father is CURIOSITY.

When you are tired of photography, you are tired of life.

New day, new image ...

Sharp lenses set **only** the upper limit of sharpness a photographer can obtain.

Your photography records your **dance** with life.

Photographic style is

personal visual culture.

Knowing what to photograph is about knowing what **not** to photograph.

Photographs illuminate
the present with
the past.

A photograph is *a* **screen-shot** of your mind's eye.

You'll miss the picture if you haven't **first** seen it in your mind.

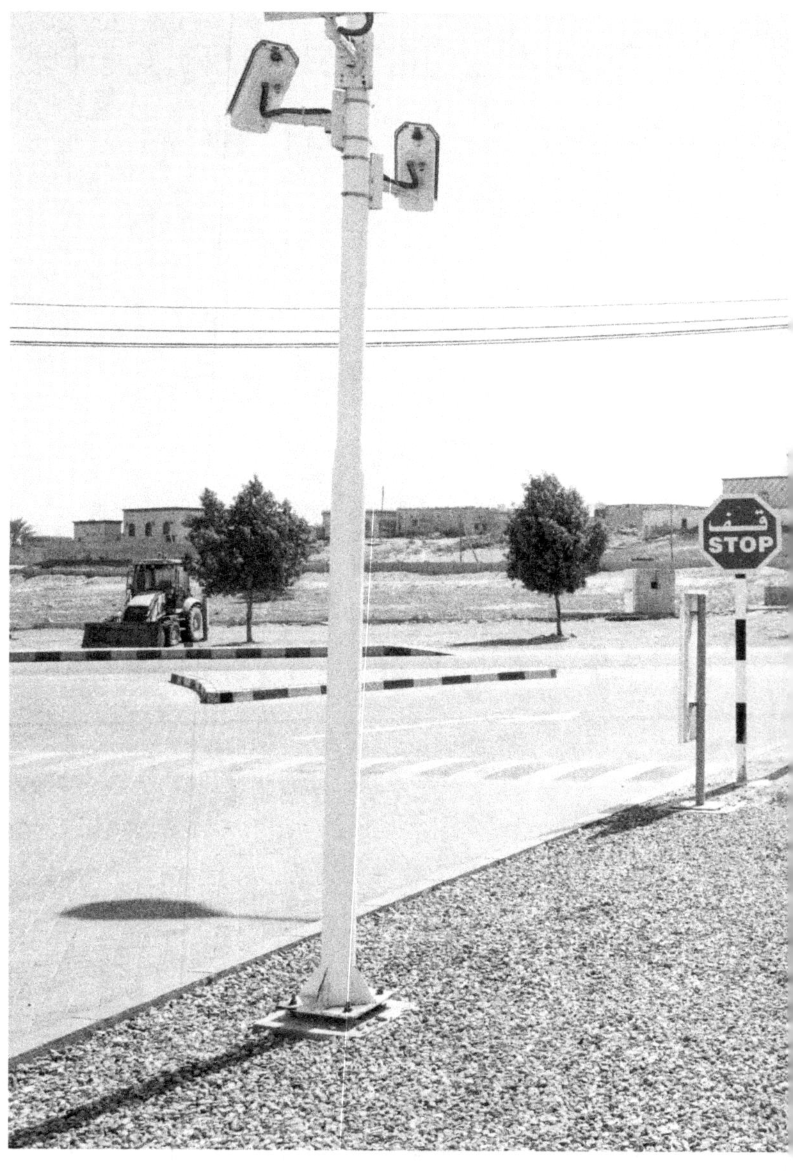

قف
STOP

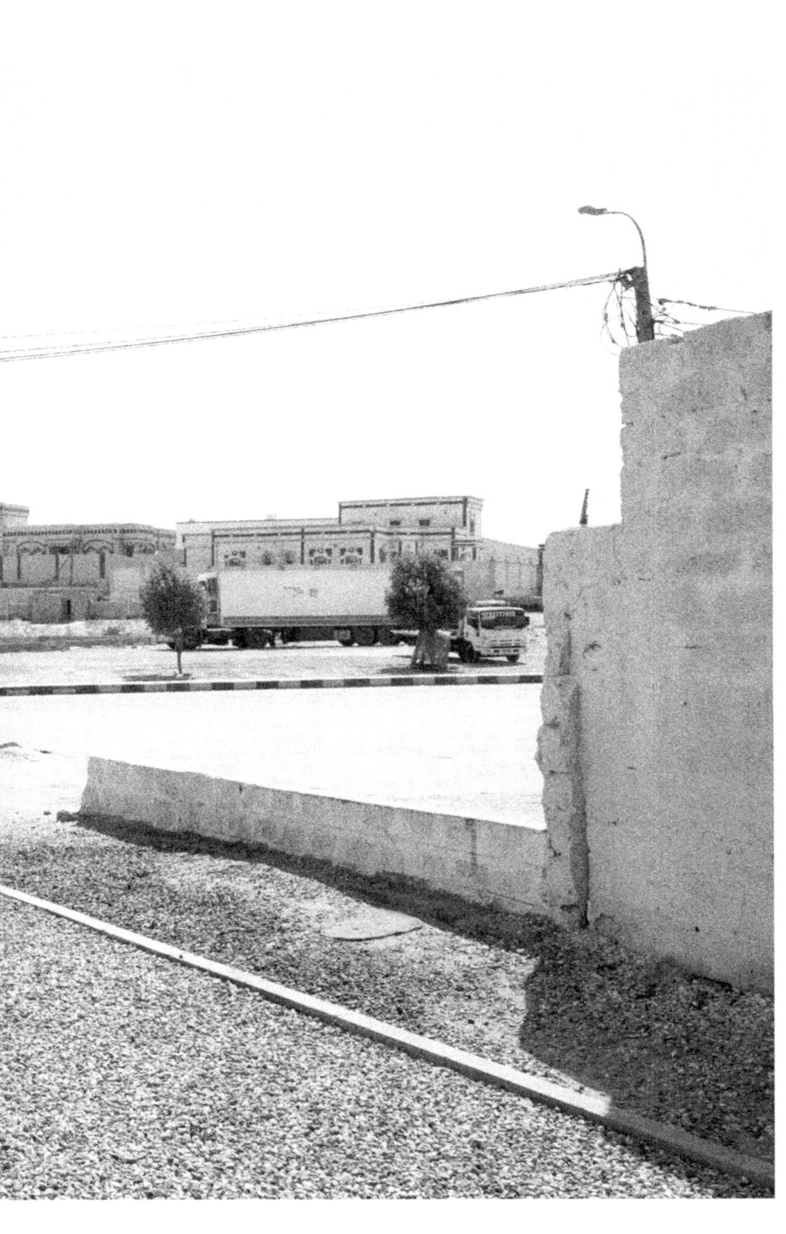

Photography is the projection of the psychical on the physical.

Photography preserves the past by creating a future out of the present.

A photograph maps the struggle between light and dark.

Imagination is to imaging
as love is to singing.

Photography's ambition
is
attention.

To photograph is to
sculpt an idea in
light.

When sight is starved of
beauty, the soul goes
hungry.

Photography
translates the
visible into
the readable.

A photograph notates the
choreography of life's
dance.

A photograph is life
thin-sliced.

LIFE PROVIDES;

we have only to open

our eyes.

Only one letter separates
'imagine' from 'imaging'.

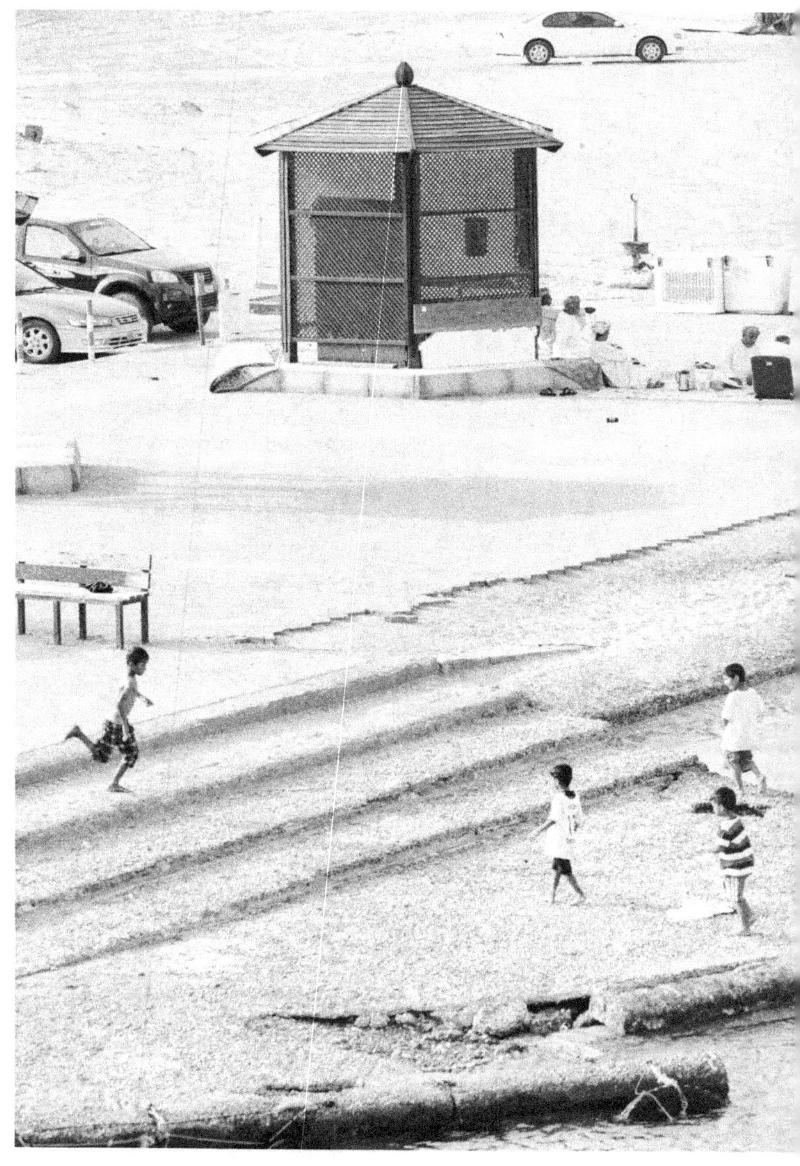

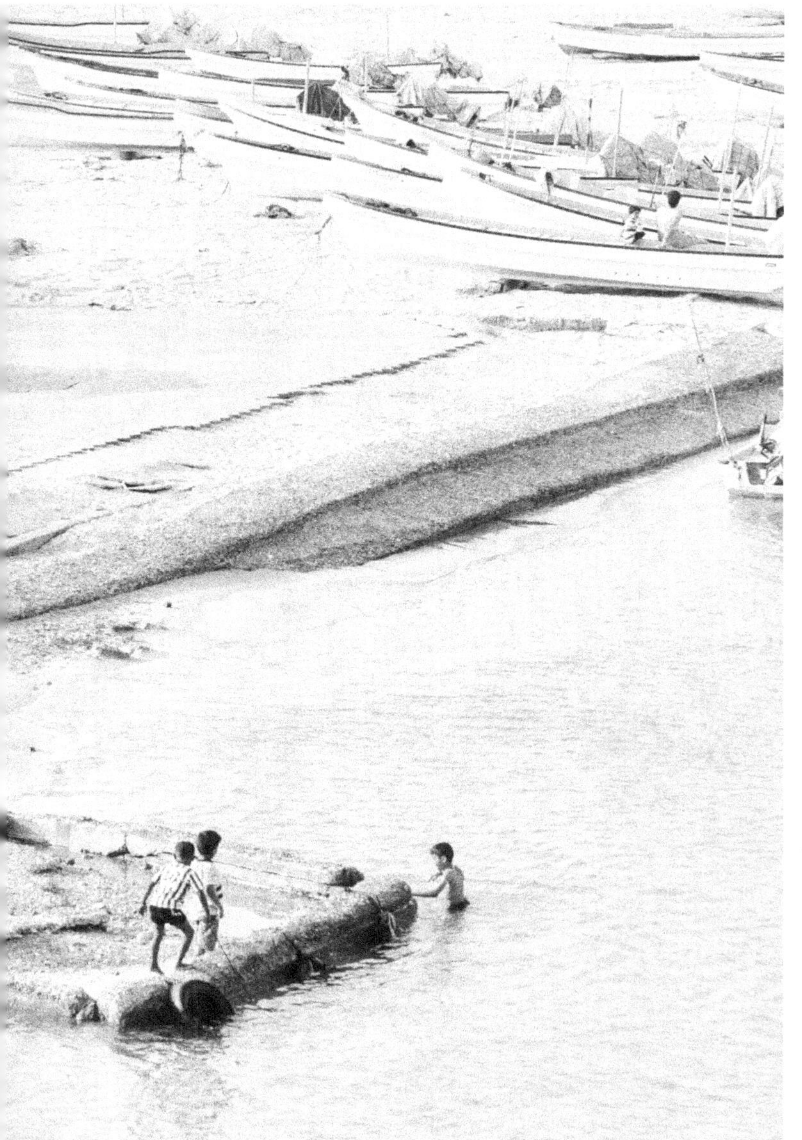

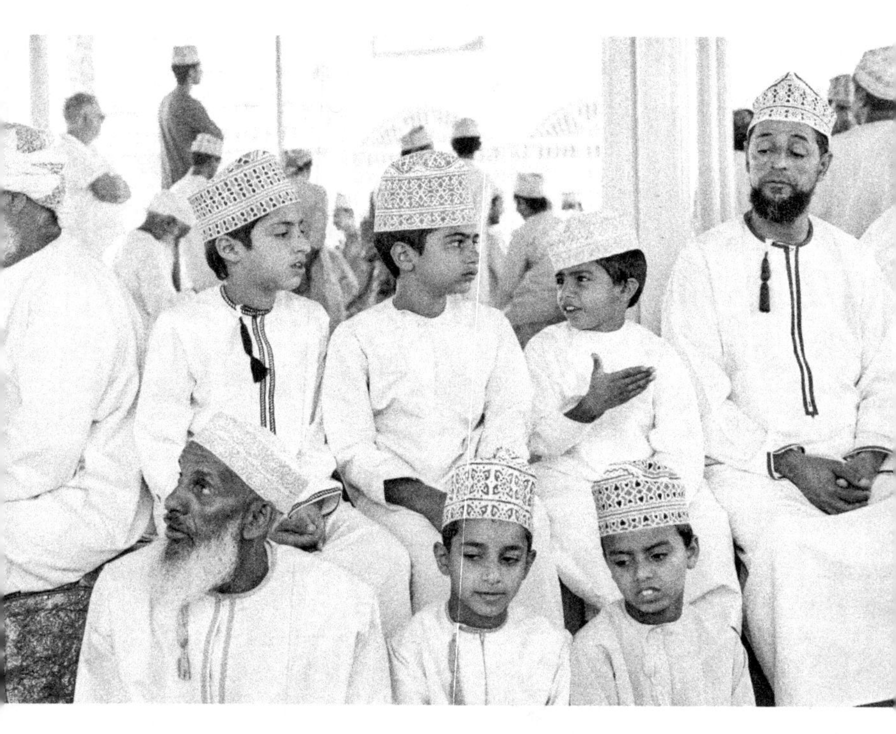

truism

If you can see,
you have
good
conditions for
photography.

For photographers, 'composition' is usually an impossibility: what we usually work with is the *disposition of things.*

Feeling
comfortable?
If so, **you're too far away.**

The best cameras can be improved by using a better lens, but even the best will capture only rubbish through a poor lens.

Image quality is **almost** entirely about what you can't measure.

Dynamism in an image arises from its internal organisation, not from any external effect.

To create, you have only to stop holding yourself back.

An **able** photographer is commander of the technique but is **not captained by the technicalities.**

If you picture in your mind **the image you want** instead of picturing the camera you want, your photography will improve, *instantly.*

What matters most of all is to approach each and every day with the knowledge that a fine image is just round the corner.

Ignoring the good-but-not-great, the also-rans, and the time-wasters , that's the hard part.

In colour photography, there are two subjects: the **subject** and the **colours.**

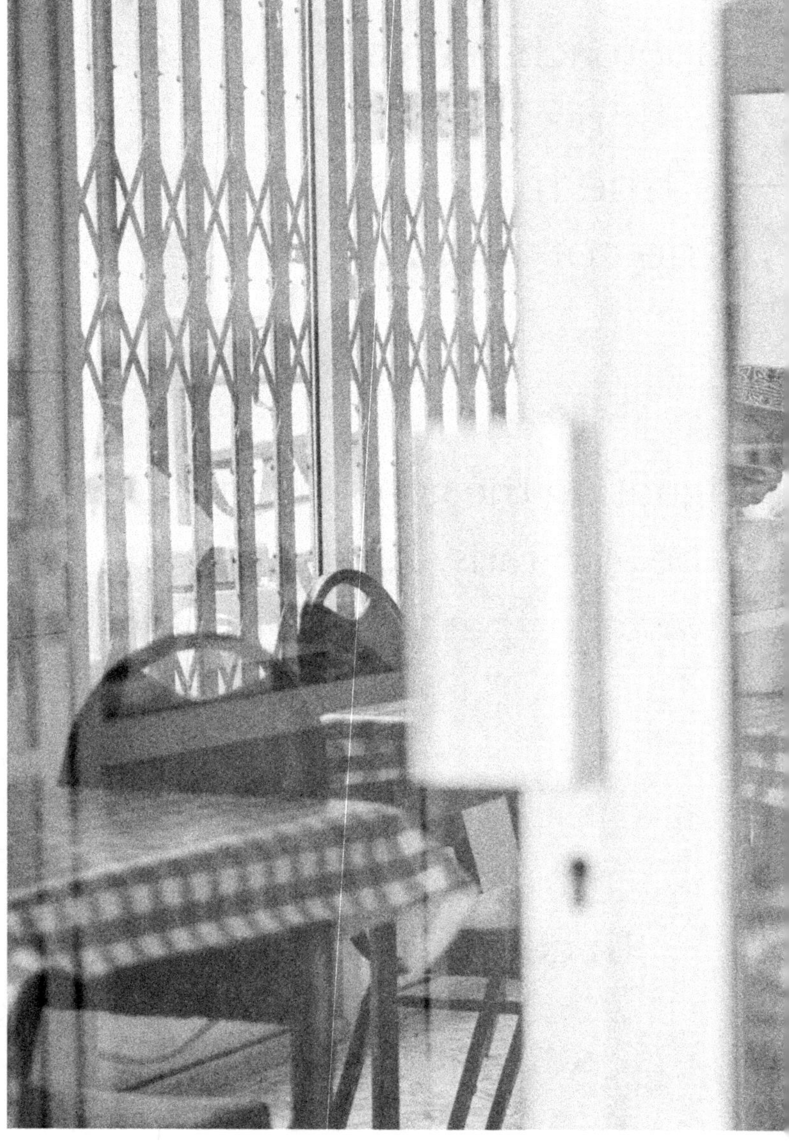

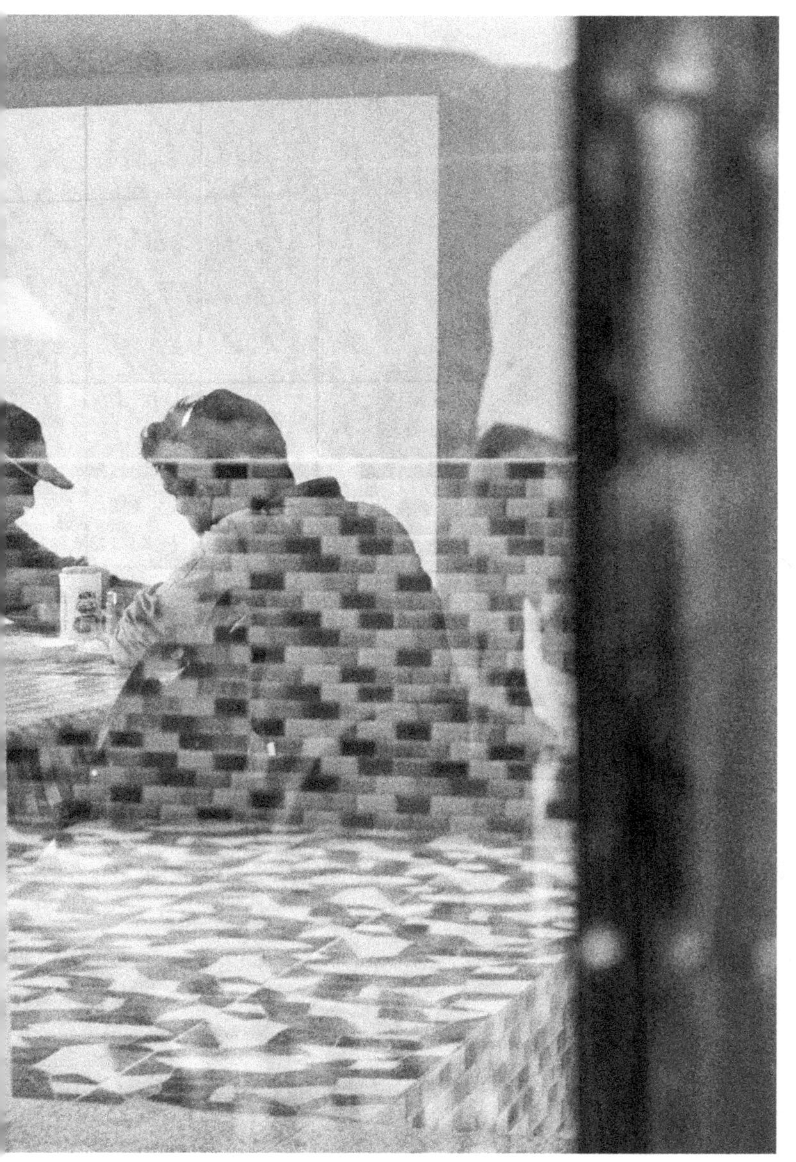

Focus defines
visual priority.

Everything
you need to know about lighting:
all **light is good** light.

If you don't know what a good
picture looks like, how do you
know what makes a bad one?

If you click the shutter without *'clicking'* with the subject, you're in the same league as traffic cameras.

Anyone can shoot sharp. What makes the difference is **where you put the blur.**

IF YOU miss a shot, there are two things you can blame: you, or yourself.

Exposure metering sets the
level of expression.

It's a very fine
photograph when
there's *nothing* to
add, nothing to
take away.

If your camera could make
better pictures in someone else's
hands, the camera is not
what is holding you back.

The more of your heart
you put into an image,
the **greater its magic.**

If you shoot to your strengths;
you don't have to worry about
your weaknesses.

IF YOU want your pictures to look
like everyone else's, follow the
same rules as they do.

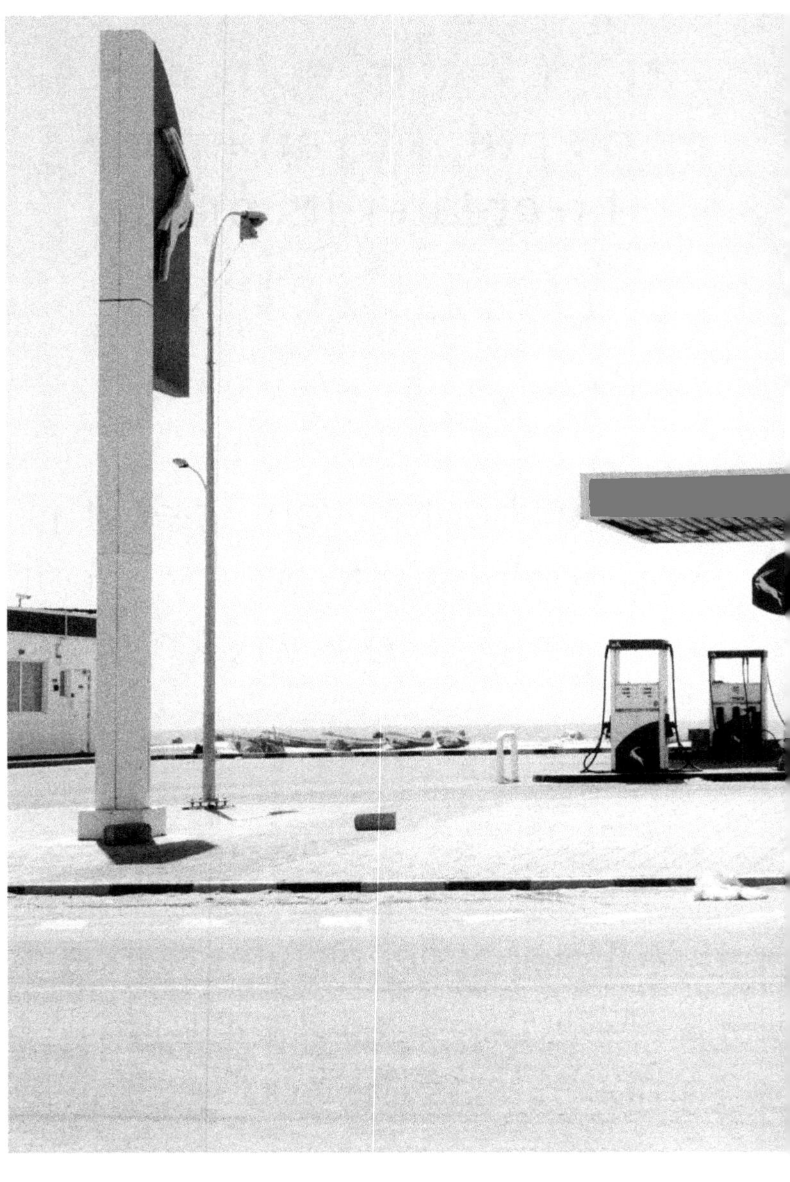

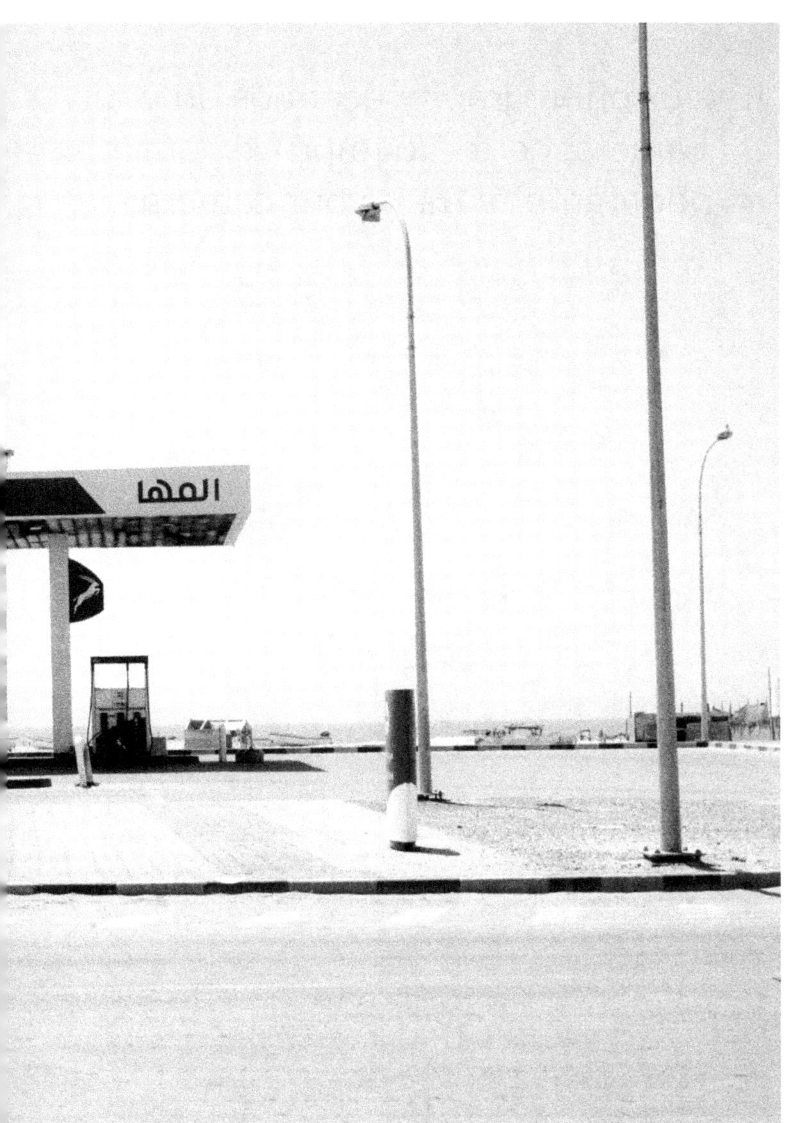

المها

If your photography depends on your camera, better to improve your photography than your camera.

We don't make stills pictures these days. We make restless images.

An image is most f l a t when every part is sharp.

Pictures are like relationships: if one takes too much effort to make work, it's not a keeper.

INSISTING on raw files is like demanding beef at every meal: hard to digest, and too much is not good for you.

IF YOU NEED to ask why you need to shoot in raw, you don't need to shoot in raw.

In photography, anything you can measure isn't important; but everything you can't measure matters.

Any camera that works is a pretty good camera.

The difference between a professional photographer and an amateur is that for one, the photograph is the beginning, for the other it's the end.

There's little point having a camera on manual mode if your brain's on auto.

Photographs are **created by being fully in the moment.** All else is distraction.

There's only *one* guarantee: if you don't try, you won't win.

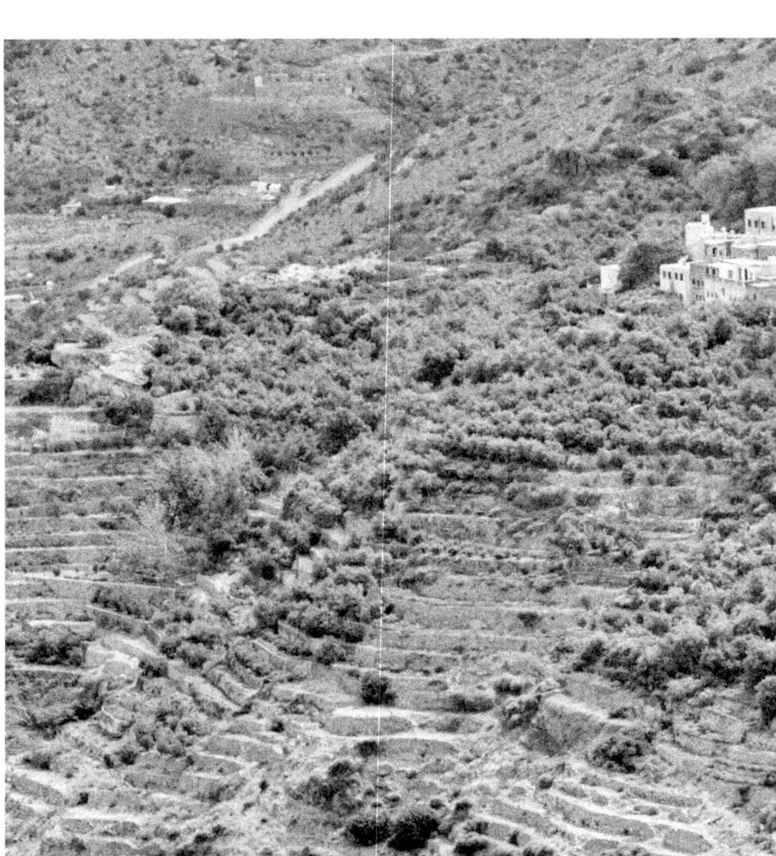

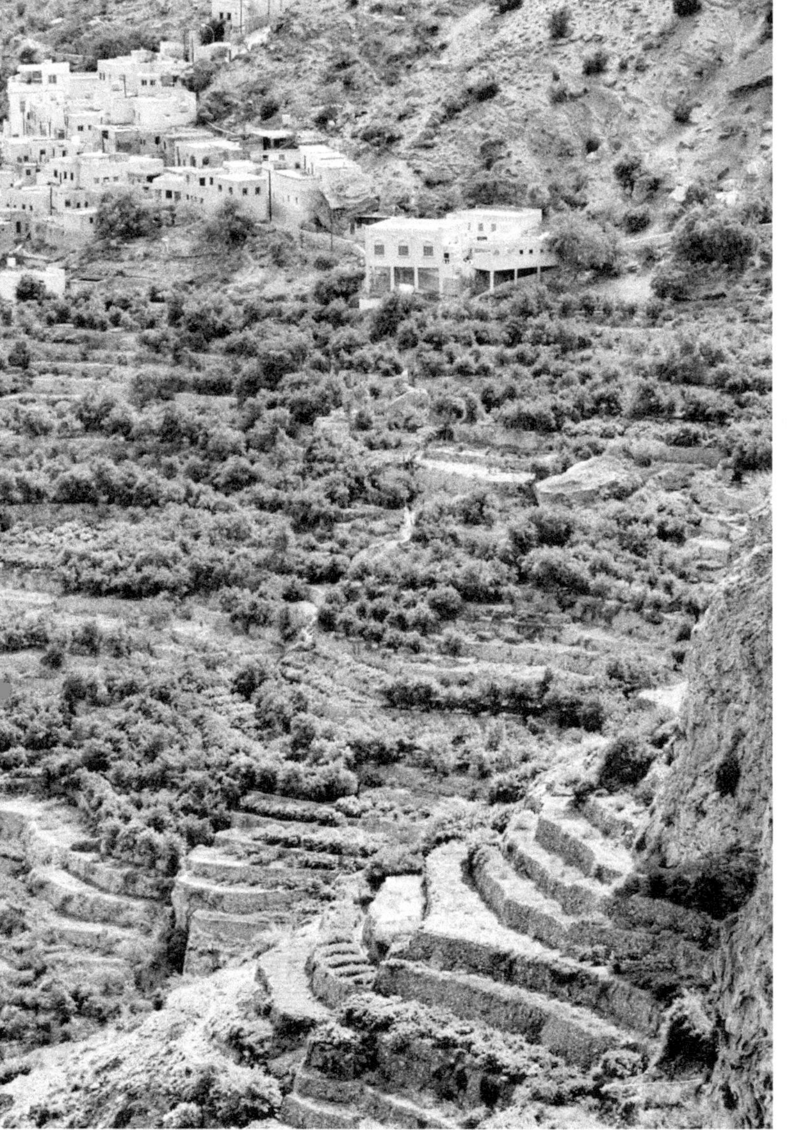

An **image** is like a loved voice heard briefly, yet the *feeling* lingers.

A **good** image will work at any size: **postage stamp to mural.**

LEARNING photography technique is how photographers **get trained by their equipment.**

COMPOSITION is ABOUT getting **heart, thought,** act and world in a **straight line.**

THE JOB of an image is not to reach out to viewers, but to **draw them in.**

The lens points **outwards** when you photograph but points inwards **when you select the image.**

If knowing how to photograph had anything to do with it, we'd make great photographs all the time.

An image is most two-dimensional when everything is sharp.

IT TAKES *A LOT* of hard work to make photography look easy; but it's easy to make it look hard work.

The search for the
perfect photograph
is a search for the **perfect
excuse for failing.**

Photography **may
not lie,** but it only ever
tells **half-truths.**

Mastery takes you **from**
'I am photographing'
to 'It is being photographed'.